EMPATH

*How to Thrive in Life as A Highly Sensitive
– Meditation Techniques to Clear Your
Energy, Shield Your Body,
and Overcome Fears*

© Copyright 2017 by Ryan James & Amy White - All rights reserved.

The following Book is reproduced below with the goal of providing information that is as accurate and as reliable as possible. Regardless, purchasing this Book can be seen as consent to the fact that both the publisher and the author of this book are in no way experts on the topics discussed within, and that any recommendations or suggestions made herein are for entertainment purposes only. Professionals should be consulted as needed before undertaking any of the action endorsed herein.

This declaration is deemed fair and valid by both the American Bar Association and the Committee of Publishers Association and is legally binding throughout the United States.

Furthermore, the transmission, duplication or reproduction of any of the following work, including precise information, will be considered an illegal act, irrespective whether it is done electronically or in print. The legality extends to creating a secondary or tertiary copy of the work or a recorded copy and is only allowed with express written consent of the Publisher. All additional rights are reserved.

The information in the following pages is broadly considered to be a truthful and accurate account of facts, and as such any inattention, use or misuse of the information in question by the reader will render any resulting actions solely under their purview. There are no scenarios in which the publisher or the original author of this work can be in any fashion deemed liable for any hardship or damages that may befall them after undertaking information described herein.

Additionally, the information found on the following pages is intended for informational purposes only and should thus be considered, universal. As befitting its nature, the information presented is without assurance regarding its continued validity or interim quality. Trademarks that mentioned are done without written consent and can in no way be considered an endorsement from the trademark holder.

Table of Contents

Introduction 1

Chapter 1: What is An Empath?... 7

Chapter 2: Coping Mechanisms for Empaths....................... 17

Chapter 3: Meditation for Empaths.. 25

Chapter 4: Meditation Techniques to Clear Negative Energy 43

Chapter 5: Meditation Techniques to Shield the Empath's Body 59

Chapter 6: Meditation Techniques to Overcome Fear 67

Chapter 7: Yoga for Empaths 81

Conclusion 101

You Also Might Be Interested In...

Empath Series Book #1

Do you feel like you are an Empath?

People who are Empaths are highly sensitive people who has the natural ability to sense and tap into the emotional and cognitive states of others. Most are born this way, although some may develop later over the course of a lifetime. Being an Empath means that you are able to deeply feel other's experiences and emotions and often times you have a hard time separating your energy from someone else's.

Being an unprotected Empath may lead to a variety of damaging and difficult feelings. You may find that these feelings can affect you physically and emotionally and this is why it is very important to learn techniques to harness and nurture your gift.

In this complete guide, we will go over everything you need to know to thrive in life as an Empath, and also as a highly sensitive. Including:

- Understanding empaths and Empathy
- Traits of an Empath
- Self-tests for Empaths
- Living life as an Empath
- Empath related problems and how to overcome them
- How to deal with negative entities
- Techniques to clear negative energy from your surroundings

- How to learn and control Empath abilities
- Chakra development for Empaths
- Emotional management techniques for Empaths

This is a lifelong guide for any sensitive person who's been told to "stop being so sensitive"

Click Here or go to:

https://www.amazon.com/Empath-Sensitive-Ultimate-Understanding-Embracing-ebook/dp/B072HF6HPX to take a look at the book.

INTRODUCTION

I want to thank you and congratulate you for purchasing the book, *"Empath: How to Thrive in Life as a Highly Sensitive – Meditation Techniques to Clear Your Energy, Shield Your Body, and Overcome Fears"*.

You know what they say – too much of something is bad for you. That is precisely the case with empaths.

Empaths are people who have too much empathy. Empaths take other people's emotions as their own. They even feel other people's emotions. This is the reason why they usually feel drained when exposed to a lot of people. They find public places overwhelming. Even just watching violence and cruelty on TV is almost always unbearable for empaths.

This is the reason that it is important for empaths to learn coping techniques that will help them shield their bodies from negative energy and overcome their fears. And this book was developed in order to help empaths protect themselves.

In this book, you'll learn:

- What an empath is and how to determine if you are one
- The challenges of being an empath
- How to thrive as an empath
- How meditation can help empaths
- Basic meditation tips
- Meditation techniques to clear negative energy
- 100 affirmations that will help ward off negative energy
- Meditation techniques that will help protect the empath's body from the physical symptoms of the people around them
- Meditation techniques that will help empaths overcome their fears.
- 70 affirmations that will help empaths overcome fears
- Meditation techniques that are specially developed for empaths
- Yoga poses for empaths

- Yoga tips for empaths

If you are an empath, the techniques you can find in this book will help you deal with the problems and challenges that you face each day. These techniques will help you create boundaries and protect yourself from negative energy, depression, anxiety, and misery.

Being an empath is a gift, but it comes at a price. This book will help you minimize the costs of being one. It will help you live a happy and peaceful life.

Thanks again for purchasing this book. I hope you enjoy it!

Your Free Gift

As a way of saying thanks for your purchase, I wanted to offer you a free bonus E-book called "*How to Talk to Anyone: 50 Best Tips and Tricks to Build Instant Rapport*".

Within this comprehensive guide, you will find information on:

- How to make a killer first impression
- Tips on becoming a great listener
- Using the FORM method for asking good questions
- Developing a great body language
- How to never run out of things to say
- Bonus chapters on Persuasion, Emotional Intelligence, and How to Analyze People

To grab your free bonus book just tap here, or go to:

http://ryanjames.successpublishing.club/freebonus/

CHAPTER 1

WHAT IS AN EMPATH?

Empaths are loving and sensitive beings who can feel and absorb other people's emotions.

Empathy -- the ability to fully understand and even feel other people's emotions -- is incredibly powerful. It allows you to connect with other people. It allows you to be kinder and more considerate to the people around you.

With empaths though, the empathy is turned up to 11. Empaths have the capacity for so much understanding that they literally feel other people's emotions. Many empaths have such strong intuition that they seemingly have the capacity to read other people's minds. They can tell when someone is being dishonest. They can read people and find out what their intentions are. They can spot even the well-crafted lies.

Empaths can connect with other people like no other. They can even heal others in a way, as they can help ease burdens. They can feel positive emotions intensely and experience periods of bliss when surrounded by happy people.

Having too much empathy can be a two-edged sword though. You see, empaths can also feel negative emotions as intensely. Having the ability to absorb other people's negative emotions can be overwhelming and it can take a toll on their physical and emotional health.

It's no surprise that many empaths suffer from a wide array of mental health issues such as depression, anxiety, chronic stress, and eating disorders. They experience panic attacks and they would most likely turn to food, drugs, and sex to ease their anxiety and pain. They also have a hard time developing relationships because they know when someone is being dishonest to them.

So you see, if you're an empath, there is a great need to clear out negative energy from your body and protect yourself.

The Unique Abilities of Empaths

Empaths are not superheroes – at least not the kind you read about in comics. But there are many things they are capable of. They can save the day by being able to spot if you're having a rough one and saying a kind word, and that's just for starters. If you have any of the following abilities, you are probably an empath:

1. Psychometry

   Did you ever feel uncomfortable in a certain place for a seemingly unexplainable reason? Do you feel something from an object you bought at a vintage shop, especially from one that looks like it has a lot of history? Do you feel that the internet or even the computer is overwhelming? Psychometry is the ability to receive energy and information from places, objects, and photograph. It allows you to feel the vibe of a specific place, food, or place.

2. Telepathy

   We're not talking about something similar to the psychic abilities you see in movies. Empaths cannot directly hear other people's thoughts, but they can sense it. So in a way, they have the ability to read other people's thoughts.

3. Mediumship

   Empaths are highly sensitive to everything around them. This is the reason that they have the ability to connect with the spiritual world. They have the hidden ability to connect with friends and family members who have passed away.

4. Emotional Healing

   Highly sensitive people like empaths can do more than sense other people's emotions. They also feel them. When they are exposed to people who are despondent, they will feel sad as well. When they are in the presence of someone under a lot of stress, they will feel the burden as well. Because they are attuned to others' suffering, they are almost always the first ones who reach out and attempt to share the burden or make the other person feel better.

5. Physical Manifestations

    This is probably one of the worst things about being an empath. You see, empaths can not only feel other people's emotions, these emotions can also manifest physically. They could feel physical pain and discomfort because of what other people are feeling.

6. Animal Communication

    Empaths are excellent animal caretakers because they are able to communicate with animals. They can feel their pet's pain and happiness. They are able to connect with animals in a deeper level. This is the reason why a lot of empaths are vegetarians.

7. Connection to Nature

    This may be hard to believe but, every living thing has "feelings", even plants. Empaths can sense whether the plant is doing well or dying.

8. Geomancy

    Do you feel drained when you are exposed to certain places? Do you feel happy when you are on a beach or high-vibe places? If you answered yes to these questions, you may be an empath.

    High vibe places are those that are associated with feelings of serenity, love, and compassion.

    Empaths have the ability to read the energy of places. They feel drained when they are in malls, marketplaces, and other low vibration places. Low vibration places are places associated with dark qualities such as depression, fear, or greed. Examples of these places include casinos and malls.

9. Pre-cognition

    Do you ever feel like you know that something's going to happen? Is your intuition so strong that you can take one look at the circumstances and then predict events? Empaths have the ability to do so.

10. Knowing or Claircognizance

Empaths just know things without knowing why they knew it. They almost always know what to do at any given moment.

Empaths absorb the energies of other people all the time. This is the reason that they feel drained when they are in crowded places.

They are also good listeners. They are highly sensitive. They are highly attuned to other people's mood- whether good or bad.

Empaths experience the world through their intuition. They have a rich inner life which is the reason why they often zone out. They can also get overwhelmed by intimate relationships.

This barrage of emotions is one of the reasons that empaths may end up feeling depressed. If you are an empath, you need to protect yourself from other people's negative energy, and you can do this through a powerful ancient practice called meditation. We will discuss that in detail in the latter chapters.

The Empath Checklist

All empaths are sensitive, but not all highly sensitive people are empaths. So how do you know if you're an empath?

Well, here's a quick quiz that summarizes what we've mentioned so far.

- Do you often feel overwhelmed when you're with a large group of people? (Yes/No)

- Can you accurately identify how other people are feeling? (Yes/No)

- Do you feel happy when you make other people happy? (Yes/No)

- Do you find yourself able to "see through" people? (Yes/No)

- Do you often feel sick when you're around sick and depressed people? (Yes/No)

- Have most of your intuitions turned out to be correct? (Yes/No)

- Do you often sacrifice your needs and happiness for other people? (Yes/No)

- Are you susceptible to constant emotional roller coasters? (Yes/No)

- Do you often hide in your room or even in the bathroom just to calm and rejuvenate yourself? (Yes/No)

- Can you sense a certain energy from things and animals? (Yes/No)

- Do people feel comfortable unloading their problems to you, even strangers? (Yes/No)

- Do you feel physical pain for other people's physical symptoms? (Yes/No)

- Do you have the ability to predict certain events? (Yes/No)

- Do you have the strong urge to help outcasts and underdogs? (Yes/No)

- Do you find violent and dramatic TV shows exhausting? (Yes/No)

- Are you creative and do you have artistic abilities? (Yes/No)

- Do you feel a wide variety of strong emotions in one day? (Yes/No)

- Can you often tell when someone is lying? (Yes/No)

- Can you read the emotions of animals? (Yes/No)

- Do you feel sick when you see violence on TV? (Yes/No)

- Are you hypersensitive to noise? (Yes/No)

- Can you sense other people's sadness? (Yes/No)

- Do you often feel that you're different from most people? (Yes/No)

If you answered yes to most of the questions, it means that you're likely an empath and you could benefit from the meditation techniques in this book.

CHAPTER 2

COPING MECHANISMS FOR EMPATHS

Like we said, being an empath can be a gift in a lot of ways.

It allows you to be some kind of a walking lie detector.

It allows you to connect with others in a much deeper level.

It enables you to function like a chameleon, adapting to different types of people and situations.

It allows you to experience intense bouts of pure bliss.

But it's not all sunshine and rainbows for empaths. It has pitfalls, too. Empaths connect with other people on a deeper level so they tend to prioritize other people's needs. They engage with people-pleasing behavior.

They avoid asking for a break and they say "I'm sorry" even when there's absolutely no apology needed. They avoid disagreements and they often get taken advantage of.

They also absorb other people's negative energy and so they feel tired and weak, almost all of the time. They also tend to lose control of their emotions because of the electrical build up that they develop from taking on other people's emotions and vibrations. Because of this, many empaths tend to avoid big crowds. They also typically use alcohol and drugs to cope and relax. Doing so allows them to escape their empathic waves.

Being an empath is extremely exhausting. It can rob you of your joy. It can keep you from living a happy and fulfilling life – the life that you truly deserve.

The good news is, you can succeed even if you are an empath through various coping mechanisms. The following are just some of the basics. More techniques will be discussed in detail in succeeding chapters.

Protect Yourself From Other People's Emotions and Energy

To prevent fatigue, depression, and mental breakdown, you have to protect yourself from other people's energy and emotion. You must try to only embrace the emotions that are yours. You can do this through meditation. A number of meditation techniques can help you build a protective shield and ward off all unwanted energies and emotions. We will discuss this later on in this book.

Eat Healthy Food

Empaths can sense the energy of food. So, you have to avoid foods that contain low vibrational energy such as white rice, coffee, genetically modified food, fish, poultry, pasteurized cow's milk, cheese, yogurt, frozen foods, deep fried foods, and sodas.

You have to eat more of high vibration foods, such as herbal teas, olive oil, coconut oil, raw chocolate, legumes, raw honey, spirulina, seeds, nuts, brown rice, spelt, amaranth, spices, organic foods, Himalayan salt, extra virgin coconut oil, cilantro, blue green algae, and teas.

Exercise Regularly

Exercising will help cleanse out all the unwanted energy. Quite the opposite, It gives you energy and makes you more resilient.

It also strengthens your body and it helps you deal with depression and anxiety. It reduces stress and increase the production of happy hormones such as serotonin and endorphins.

Exercise also helps you focus. It improves your memory and cognitive function.

Realize That You Have The Power To Reject Other People's Energy

If you pick up emotions and energies that are not yours, you allow their vibration to influence yours. This means that other people's vibration cannot affect you if you will not allow it. If you are happy and someone is angry, you cannot pick up that anger unless you permit it.

The only way to avoid absorbing other people's negative emotions is to raise your vibrational energy. You can do this being more conscious of your thoughts. You need to focus on positive thoughts and ward off negative thoughts. You can also increase your vibrational energy by practicing random acts of kindness and by exercising regularly. When you do something good for other people, you'll instantly feel elated.

Say Positive Affirmations

Saying positive affirmations increases your self-esteem and raises your vibrational energy. It trains your mind to focus on positive thoughts. Each morning, look at the mirror and say positive affirmations. This book contains 150 affirmations.

Practice Visualization

Your mind is so powerful that it could shape your external reality. Visualizing a protective light around you can actually help you ward off negative emotions and energies.

Visualization is also an extremely relaxing technique that can help relieve stress and anxiety. It increases your focus and it also boosts your self-confidence, raising your vibrational frequency.

Learn to Forgive

If you're an empath, you've probably been taken advantage of a lot of times. This could lead to resentment and hidden anger. To live a happy life as an empath, you have to learn to forgive even those who took advantage of you.

Maintain an Attitude of Gratitude

Gratitude brings more into your life. It increases your resilience and it allows you to focus on the bright side of things. It also raises vibrational frequency and helps you ward off negative energies.

Do Not Take Responsibilities That Are Not Yours

You have to drop your people-pleasing habit and learn to say no to requests that you are not comfortable with. This will prevent you from spreading yourself too thin. It also keeps other people from taking advantage of your gentle and helpful nature.

Take a Break from Social Media

The social media, or the internet in general, can be toxic. To protect your energy, turn off your computer and take a walk around your neighborhood after work. Do not check your phone unless someone is calling you. This habit can help clear toxic energy and improve your peace of mind.

Avoid Toxic People and Places

Some places like malls are naturally toxic. To effectively cope with being an empath, you have to avoid toxic places and go to high vibrational places like the beach, churches, or the park.

You have to avoid toxic people, too – those who try to belittle and criticize you. It's quite easy to spot toxic people because you'll feel exhausted, tired, and drained after talking you them or standing close to them. Toxic people are judgmental, inconsistent, manipulative, and fake. Stay away from these people as much as you can.

Being an empath comes with a lot of challenges. But, you can still build a happy and successful life by protecting yourself from negative energies, practicing self-care, and surrounding yourself with people who love and respect you.

CHAPTER 3

MEDITATION FOR EMPATHS

There are many tools that empaths can use to protect their energy and achieve peace of mind and meditation is one of the most powerful.

Meditation goes way back to 1500 BCE. It is practiced by many spiritual techniques. It originated from India, but it is now practiced in different parts of the world.

Meditation is usually associated with spirituality. This practice has strong spiritual roots and it was practiced by spiritual mystics and monks. However, meditation has become a secular practice and it is now practiced by people from all walks of life. It is a practice that everyone can do and everyone can benefit from, including empaths.

Benefits of Meditation

A number of studies show that meditation has a number of remarkable benefits. For starters, it decreases your levels of anxiety, depression, and stress. It also reduces the symptoms of various health conditions such as asthma, chronic pain, high blood pressure, heart disease, insomnia, tension headaches, irritable bowel syndrome, diabetes, and brain diseases. It improves cognitive function and memory. It slows down aging, too.

Meditation can benefit empaths in a lot of ways, including:

1. It improves concentration.

    If you're an empath, you are distracted all the time by the energies around you. Meditation improves your focus and helps you tune out all the thoughts and energies that you do not need at that moment.

2. It encourages you to adopt a healthy lifestyle.

    Empaths usually develop unhealthy habits to cope with overwhelming emotions. Meditation helps you eliminate these healthy habits. It helps you stop smoking and give up drugs, alcohol, and unhealthy foods.

3. It increases self-awareness.

    Empaths often lose their sense of self because they listen to all the external noises around them day in and day out. Meditation helps you get in touch with your inner self and remember who you really are.

4. It increases happiness.

    Meditation increases the activity in the left side of the prefrontal cortex, which is responsible for positive emotions.

5. It increases mental strength.

    Empaths are easily swayed or distracted by thoughts and emotions including those that are not theirs. If you're an empath, you can greatly benefit from meditation because it increases mental fortitude. It increases your ability to bounce back from difficult circumstances and boosts your self-confidence. Regular meditation practice gives you the strength to establish a personal boundary and embrace change.

6. It helps you ward off other people's symptoms.

   If you're an empath, you frequently absorb other people's symptoms, so much so that you could feel sick whenever you're exposed to sick people. This could prevent you from enjoying life to the fullest. Meditation can help build a protective layer that protects you from other people's symptoms.

7. Meditation rejuvenates your body and mind.

   Empaths are often tired because they have to deal with external noise all the time. That can be draining and overwhelming. Meditation can help you deal with that because it refreshes your mind and body.

8. Meditation allows you to experience something really rare – peace of mind.

   Peace is something that seems unachievable for an empath. Meditation helps you achieve peace of mind by silencing all the noise in your head. This works even during challenging times.

It helps you gain clarity. It helps you achieve a state of mental calmness. It allows you to experience a strong sense of freedom and happiness.

9. It gives you the courage to overcome your fears.

   Being exposed to negative emotions all the time can lead to doubts, anxiety, and fears. Fear is a crippling emotion. It can keep you from taking risks and living the life that you deserve. It can lead to indecisiveness that leads to most lethal states of all – stagnation.

Meditation also keeps you young. It strengthens your immune system and your heart. It decreases the symptoms of various health issues such as depression, anxiety, auto-immune diseases, ADHD, asthma, inflammatory disorders, menopausal syndrome, brain problems, and pre-menstrual syndrome.

All in all, meditation clarifies your mind, allowing you to thrive in this world.

There are many types of meditation, namely: zazen, vipassana, mindfulness, loving kindness meditation, mantra meditation, transcendental meditation, kundalini meditation, and chakra meditation. This book contains techniques that combine different meditation types. These techniques are specially created for empaths.

Meditation Tips for Empaths

Empaths struggle with internal and external noise all the time. This is the reason why meditation can be extremely challenging for empaths.

Meditation is not easy, but it is something that you can master over time. Here's a list of tips and techniques that will help you get started:

1. Commit yourself to the meditation practice.

   Meditation is not something that you can master in 30 minutes. It is a practice that you have to do daily. To reap all the benefits meditation, you have to commit yourself to it and incorporate it into your daily schedule.

2. Wear comfortable clothing.

    Tight clothes are distracting. You want to be as comfortable as possible when you are meditating so wear loose and comfortable clothes.

3. Create a meditation space.

    Create a space in your home where you can practice meditation. Make sure that space is clean. You can decorate that space with energy clearing tools such as scented candles, incense, and crystals. Scented candles can help you focus so it would help if you light one or two when you're meditating.

4. Start small.

    Set your meditation time to two to five minutes each day on your first week. Then, you can increase your meditation time as you progress. Be careful with this because if you're too ambitious in setting your meditation goals, you'd get disappointed and you'll end up giving up your meditation practice.

5. Cleanse your body before cleansing your mind.

   Meditation is a powerful spiritual practice. So, you have to cleanse your body first before you start cleansing your mind. You can do this by taking a bath before meditation. You can also do this by doing simple cleansing yoga poses such as the tree pose, easy pose, boat pose, camel pose, and the supported shoulder stand.

6. Consult your doctor before trying an advanced meditation technique.

   The meditation techniques contained in this book are basic. But, if you decide to practice advanced techniques such as kundalini meditation later on, it's best to consult your doctor especially if you're suffering from a mental health problem such as depression.

   Do not meditate right after eating as this may affect your ability to focus. And most importantly, be kind to yourself. It's impossible to master meditation in just a few hours, days, and weeks. Be patient.

Meditation Tools for Empaths

Meditation is a powerful relaxation technique. But, if you're an empath, you'll need tools to help you reap the maximum benefits of meditation.

Crystals

Crystals are beautiful and colorful. They have strong healing properties. They have the ability to remove stress and tension from your body. They can subtly change your health, energy, and aura.

Crystals can do a lot of things – they can increase your ability to forgive yourself and others. These crystals can remove the emotional blockages caused by fear and self-doubt. These crystals balance your energy so they're considered as first rate meditation tools. These crystals calm your mind and help you reap the full benefits of meditation.

- Rose Quartz

    Rose quartz is known as the crystal of love. This beautiful pink precious stone carries a soft, feminine energy that exudes love, compassion, and peace. If you're an empath, finding true love can be a challenge so this stone could greatly benefit you. The rose quartz also inspires you to practice self-love and put yourself above anyone else's need.

This stone heals your heart chakra and it has a strong purifying effect that flushes out all the heartaches and negative energies. It also balances the yin-yang energy in your body and improves your overall mental well-being.

- Malachite

    This has a healing energy that removes emotional blockages. It protects your core being, especially during challenging times.

- Amethyst

    Many empaths have strong intuition and yet, they do not trust this intuition most of the time. This beautiful purple stone heightens an empath's intuition and encourages them to trust their gut feelings.

- Black Tourmaline

    This has a powerful protective energy that pushes all the negative energy away. This stone is an important stone that empathic healers must have.

- Blue Topaz

    Many empaths feel that their needs are not as important as the needs of the people around them. This stone helps you think clearly and it empowers you communicate your personal truth. It helps you see the big picture and remove the tension and stress caused by relationships, work, or social interactions.

- Lapis Lazuli

    This beautiful blue stone has an intense color and appearance. It also has an intense protective power that can guard you from negative energies. This stone will help you not to take things personally and it helps clear your mind.

- Unakite

  Your emotions can be overwhelming sometimes and this can take a toll on your physical and emotional health. Unakite is a rare stone that can help balance your emotions. It also helps you connect with the Energy Source and improve your spirituality.

- Purple Jade

  This is a great protective stone for empaths because it aligns and balances your energy, keeping the negative energies in check.

Essential Oils

The aroma of essential oils can help reset your body and strengthen your spirit. It can also help create a peaceful atmosphere during meditation. Here's a list of essential oils that you can use when you're meditating:

- Lavender

  Lavender has a mesmerizing sweet scent that you can't get enough of. It helps improve your mood and improves your sleep. This oil is also useful for empaths who suffer from neurological issues such as stress, depression, and anxiety. You can spray this oil around your room before your meditation practice. You can use it as a perfume, too.

- Cedarwood

    Cedarwood has a fresh scent. It has a cooling and calming effect on the body. This oil reduces the symptoms of stress, depression, and anxiety. Its scent also induces the release of a happy hormone called serotonin, making you feel giddy, relaxed, and happy.

- Sandalwood

    If you feel anxious all the time, it would be beneficial to use sandalwood essential oil during your meditation practice. This oil also helps prevent mental sluggishness and increase your alertness. This oil improves your cognitive function, too, and protects you from dementia. It decreases the symptoms of depression, too.

- Patchouli

    This oil helps ward off negative feelings such as anger, anxiety, and sadness. It is also a powerful sedative. It helps you relax and sleep after a long tiring day.

- Basil

    Basil increases your mental alertness and decreases the symptoms of anxiety. It decreases mental fatigue, depression, and migraines. It helps you achieve clarity and increase your mental strength.

- Chamomile

    This raises your spirits and helps you fight depression. It also reduces mental sluggishness and nervousness.

- Bergamot

    This oil is a powerful relaxant. It helps relieve stress, tension, and anxiety. It also helps cure depression.

- Ylang ylang

    If you're looking for a feel-good oil, this is it. This essential oil is a natural remedy for depression. It expands your heart and it helps you release negative emotions such as anger and jealousy. It also increases your self-esteem. It also increases your self-awareness and promotes self-love.

- Rose

    This essential oil is a potent aphrodisiac and it helps improve one's self-confidence, self-esteem, and mental strength.

- Ginger

    Ginger oil increases your energy. It is a powerful remedy for the emotional and mental issues that empaths go through such as depression, stress, restlessness, anxiety, and mental exhaustion.

- Lemon

    Lemon essential oil increases your energy and it helps curb your appetite so it keeps you from turning to food when you're stressed.

- Rosemary

    This one can do wonders to your mental health. It reduces oxidative stress and it increases your mental clarity. It helps you become more decisive and less overwhelmed by life's small challenges.

- Frankincense

    Frankincense relieves stress and help fight anxiety. It increases your spiritual connection and it also strengthens your intuition. When you feel overwhelmed, this oil reduces and stabilizes your heart rate.

- Tea Tree

    Tea Tree oil has anti-cancer benefits. It is powerful because it removes the malignancy of the plasma tracts or chakras. It helps restore the natural vibrational frequency of your chakras.

- Geranium

    This oil reduces the symptoms of depression and stress. It calms your nerves and relaxes your mind.

- Eucalyptus

    Empaths are prone to mental exhaustion. Eucalyptus can help them deal with that because this oil has a refreshing and cooling effect. It is also a stimulant which helps remove mental sluggishness and exhaustion. So, if you are tired after a day of dealing with different people at work, use eucalyptus oil during our meditation practice.

- Neroli

    Neroli is a great aphrodisiac. But it does more than awaken your sexuality and bring back the wild moments of your youth. This oil releases anxiety and depression. It is a powerful tool that can help you relax during meditation.

- Cinnamon

    Empaths usually feel tired all the time because of all that negative energy that they get from people around them. This is the reason why cinnamon oil is beneficial for empaths. This essential oil increases your energy and it also strengthens your immune system and it helps treat depression, too.

- Citronella

    Citronella oil is primarily known as a repellant. But, it also has a powerful anti-anxiety because it relieves negative feelings. This oil induces strong feelings of hope and happiness.

- Geranium

    Geranium is a beautiful summer flower. This oil is a commonly used in aromatherapy. It is used for holistic treatment. Geranium reduces depression and relieves stress. It also decreases nervous tension and promotes strong feelings of well-being and peace.

Meditation is a powerful tool that you can use to achieve peace of mind. It is a tool that you can use to silence the noise around you. It allows you to make better decisions. It also enables you to build an energetic shield that protects you from all the negativity around you. It is a powerful technique that you can use to take back control in your life and protect yourself from all the unpleasant things in the world.

CHAPTER 4

MEDITATION TECHNIQUES TO CLEAR NEGATIVE ENERGY

Over time, the negative energy you constantly absorb from other people can lead to serious problems such as depression and anxiety. It can even result to mental breakdown.

To save your sanity and prevent a possible nervous breakdown, you should practice meditation regularly. The following meditation techniques can help you clear the negative energy all over your body:

Chakra Meditation to Clear Negative Energy

To begin, sit in the lotus position. If this is too hard for you, you can simply sit on a chair. Close your eyes and allow your body to relax. Let go of all the tension in your body.

Now, take a deep breath. Keep taking deep breaths and let negative thoughts float away as you inhale and exhale. Notice how your body is getting more and more relaxed with each breath. You will begin to feel peace within you. Your muscles will relax and you'll begin to feel good about yourself and everything around you.

Now, close your eyes and imagine an electric cord at your root chakra, which is located at the base of your spine. Imagine that this cord extends down through the floor and going through to the soil and into the center of the planet, connecting you to the source of energy.

As you begin to feel that strong connection with Mother Earth, focus your attention on your crown chakra which is located on your forehead. Notice how it becomes more open and how it becomes wider and wider.

Now, imagine that there's a beautiful and bright light from the sky going through your crown chakra. Feel your connection with the Higher Energy. Now, you are connected with everything below you and everything above you. Take a moment to really feel that connection running through your veins and every part of your body.

Bring your attention to your heart chakra which is located at the center of your chest. Imagine that there is a bowl in your heart chakra. This bowl is filled with light of love. It is filled with light coming from your higher self -- your true self.

Now, as you breathe, imagine that this light is growing bigger and bigger. Imagine that the light is overflowing from the bowl and expanding into every cell of your body. This light comes from your heart and your higher self and it becomes brighter and brighter. It releases all the stagnant and blocked energy in your body. This light glows brighter and brighter each day. Now, let go of everything that does not serve you. Embrace who you are.

Visualize a gold magical broom in front of you. Use this magical broom to sweep away all the negative energy and tension in your body. Also, use this broom to clear out all the negative thoughts in your mind and all the negative energy that you've contracted from people that you were in contact with. Sweep your mind, neck, shoulders, all the way to your spine. Sweep away all the energy that is lower than what you choose to hold. Keep sweeping using your magical broom. Everything that you sweep away falls down to the floor and into the center of the Earth and converts into a higher vibration energy.

Continue to sweep all the negative energy and thoughts that you are willing to let go of, your thoughts and feelings. Remove all the thoughts and energy that you are willing to release.

Take a big cleansing breath. You'll feel lighter like a heavy load was just lifted out of your shoulders.

Imagine that the light from your heart continues to expand and fill your body. This light does not only clear all the negative energy in your body, it also protects your body from the negative energies of the people around you.

Affirmation Meditation to Let Go of Negative Emotions

Carrying negative emotions, especially those that are not yours can be overwhelming. It is extremely tiring. To cope with life as an empath, you must release these negative emotions regularly using meditation.

Storing negative emotions in your body can potentially harm your health. It can also disrupt your mental health and can cause issues such as anxiety, stress, and sadness. It can also weaken your body's immune system and lead to various symptoms such as stiff neck, shortness of breath, light-headedness, headaches, constipation, change in appetite, fatigue, palpitations, and upset stomach.

This may come as a surprise, but affirmations or positive words can help let go of negative emotions. When you say positive words, you'd feel positive emotions and you'll release positive energy. These emotions and energy are strong enough to trample and release all the negative emotions that you've been holding in your body.

To do this, sit in a comfortable position. Now, start to take deep breaths. Breathe in and breathe out. Breathe in all positive emotions and breathe out all negative emotions.

Close your eyes, and say these affirmations silently (if you have a hard time saying these affirmations silently, you can recite them loudly):

- *I am at peace with myself.*
- *I am comfortable with myself.*
- *I do not allow other people to dictate my worth.*
- *I block other people's emotions.*
- *I only focus on my own emotions.*
- *My mind has the power to create whatever I want to conceive.*
- *I am grateful.*
- *I welcome all peaceful thoughts into my life.*
- *I do not accept all thoughts and energies that may harm me.*
- *I am open to becoming the best that I can be.*
- *I am grateful for all the blessings in my life.*
- *I am only willing to feel the emotions that are mine.*
- *I only carry positive thoughts and feelings.*
- *I have a strong auric boundary.*
- *I protect myself from other people's feelings.*
- *I am letting go of all the thoughts and feelings that are not mine.*
- *I am letting go of all the negative emotions in my body.*
- *I can clearly communicate my needs.*
- *I am always safe and protected.*
- *I acknowledge all my emotions, but I am letting go of all the bad ones.*

- *I welcome positivity into my life.*
- *Other people cannot control my emotions, I do.*
- *I release the things that no longer serve me.*
- *I accept and appreciate myself unconditionally.*
- *I am a channel of peace.*
- *I am surrounded by positive energy.*
- *I am not afraid to express myself.*
- *I give and receive love and peace.*
- *My life is a gift.*
- *I nourish my body with healthy meals.*
- *I know that I am provided for.*
- *I have all the answers to my questions.*
- *Nothing can stop me.*
- *I am courageous.*
- *My life is an exciting adventure.*
- *I am energized.*
- *I create my own luck.*
- *I am in charge of my life.*
- *I am the source of happiness.*
- *I am wise.*
- *I honor my empathic gifts.*
- *I respect myself.*
- *I treat myself as lovingly as I can.*
- *I meditate each day to clear away all the negative energies and emotions in my body.*

- *I protect myself from all the draining energy around me.*
- *I give myself permission to recharge after a draining social activity.*
- *I am proud that I am a loving and sensitive person.*
- *I do not deny my own sensitivity.*
- *I have the ability to survive in this big world.*
- *I am always safe.*
- *I am divinely protected at all times.*
- *I let go of all my worries and problems.*
- *A big river of compassion washes away all my fears and worries.*
- *I am guided by the Spirit.*
- *I forgive all those who harmed me in the past.*
- *I let go all of the negative energy that I have contracted from the people around me.*
- *I am a powerhouse.*
- *I radiate charm and grace.*
- *I woke up today with clarity in my mind.*
- *My life is just beginning.*
- *I focus on the positive in all situations, even the painful ones.*
- *I do my best to think only positive thoughts each day.*
- *I embrace my loving and sensitive nature.*

- *I do not allow other people to take advantage of my kind nature.*
- *I harbor empowering and positive thoughts.*
- *I have healthy and abundant thoughts.*
- *I feel my thoughts with positive beliefs.*
- *I choose to think positively.*
- *I listen to my thoughts and I let go of thoughts that no longer serve me.*
- *I am forever positive.*
- *I do not tolerate negative behavior.*
- *I protect myself from energy vampires and toxic people.*
- *I approach each challenge with a smile.*
- *It is okay to recharge and stay away from people every once in a while.*
- *I experience life in a positive way.*
- *I choose to feel good.*
- *I choose to be the best that I can be.*
- *I make positive choices each day.*
- *I focus my thoughts on all the good things in my life.*
- *I sweep away all the tension from my body.*
- *I have no room for negative energy.*
- *I stay away from toxic people.*
- *I surround myself with people who lift me up.*
- *I choose to keep only the emotions that are mine.*

- *I protect myself from people who try to exploit my kind nature.*
- *I let go of my anger and resentment.*
- *I let go of all the emotions that are not mine.*
- *I have no space for negativity.*
- *I feed my mind with positive thoughts all day long.*
- *I have the power to build a life that I deserve.*
- *My needs are important, too.*
- *I always put myself first.*
- *I am worthy of all the good things in life.*
- *I remove all the hatred and resentment in my heart.*
- *My life is filled with love.*
- *I surround myself with inspiring people.*
- *I stay away from people who radiate negative energy.*
- *I am powerful.*
- *I embrace my sensitivity.*
- *I take my power back.*
- *I am stronger than my fears.*
- *I will overcome my fears.*
- *I am fearless.*
- *I am becoming more and more confident every day.*
- *I am determined.*
- *Confidence is natural to me.*
- *I am free from irrational and destructive fears.*

- *I feel more alive.*
- *I bravely protect my happiness.*
- *I am not afraid of success or failure.*
- *I release all my irrational fears.*
- *I am open to success and happiness.*
- *I am grounded.*
- *I surround myself with people who make me feel safe.*
- *All is well in my world.*
- *I have the power to overcome my fears.*
- *I am free of all fears.*
- *I release all the stress in my life.*
- *I solve my problems successfully.*
- *I have a wonderful life.*

Continue to breathe. Feel the positive energy around you. As you breathe in and breathe out, notice that you are becoming stronger and empowered.

Open your eyes and recite a short prayer of gratitude. You can simply look up to the sky and say, "thank you".

For a lot of people, it is hard to remember these affirmations. You can just pick out the affirmations that feel right for you. You don't have to say all of them. You can even create your own positive affirmations.

You can also record yourself saying these affirmations and then listen to that recording when you are meditating.

Mantra Meditation to Clear Your Energy

Mantra meditation is a meditation type that requires you to repeat a positive statement over and over during your meditation session. It is an ancient Buddhist meditation technique that has a relaxing effect in your body. It is practiced by a lot of successful people, including Fortune 500 CEOs.

This meditation technique aligns your left brain with your right brain. It also helps you become a better version of yourself. You can also use this meditation type to ward off all the negative energy around you.

1. To do this, sit in a comfortable position. You can sit in a lotus or cross-legged position or you can simply sit on a chair. Close your eyes and take deep breaths. Focus on your breath

and release all the other thoughts that may enter your mind.

2. Now, as you breathe in, say these words "I let go of all the negative energies and tension in my body".

3. As you breathe out, say these words "I only entertain thoughts that are mine". Keep repeating these mantras for about five minutes as you continue to breathe. Set a timer, so you'd know when to stop.

4. When the time is up, say a short silent prayer of thanks and then, open your eyes. You can meditate for five minutes a day during your first few weeks and then, you can gradually increase your meditation time as you progress.

Energy Cleansing Meditation

A lot of empaths are struggling with fatigue, depression, and anxiety. This energy cleansing meditation practice helps cleanse your aura and get rid of all the negative energy around you. It's best to do this meditation technique at night before bedtime.

1. Sit in a comfortable position. Breathe deeply, from your stomach, and then breathe out. You'll notice that start to relax.

2. Visualize that there's a golden light on top of your head. Now, this light flows to your head, neck, shoulders, torso, stomach, arms, and down to your hips, legs, ankles, and feet. This light flows down to the ground, connecting you firmly to the Earth.

3. This warm and glistening golden light shines and cleanses your aura. This energy helps you stay calm and it wards off all the negative energy around you.

4. Take a deep breath and as you breathe out, release all the worries, anger, anxiety, sorrow, desperation, insecurities, and grief. Keep breathing as you release all these negative energies and emotions. Take time to look inside yourself and check if there's still negative energy left. Take another deep

breath and release all the remaining negative emotions and energy within you.

5. Feel a strong sense of peace within you and around you. Nothing could destroy that peace. You are protected and safe from all the toxic energies in the world.

6. Open your eyes and say a silent prayer of thanks.

CHAPTER 5

MEDITATION TECHNIQUES TO SHIELD THE EMPATH'S BODY

Some empaths absorb other people's illness and symptoms. These people are called "physical empaths".

Physical empaths are prone to empathic illnesses. This means that they absorb other people's physical symptoms just by interacting with them or sitting next to them. They feel other people's pain and anxiety. They feel uneasy and sick in crowds. They are chronically tired and they often feel overwhelmed by the world. They also routinely have unexplained symptoms.

If you're a physical empath, it's necessary to protect yourself from stress. You need to say "no" to requests that may harm your physical and mental health. You need to create healthy boundaries and limit. You can also protect yourself from other people's illnesses, by practicing the following meditation techniques.

Mindfulness Body Scan

This mindfulness meditation technique is used by many physical therapists to treat patients with paralysis or injuries. It increases your awareness of your body and makes you more aware of the sensations in the body. It allows you to appreciate your body and it keeps you grounded, too.

To do this, lie down on your yoga mat or on your bed. Close your eyes and listen to the sound of your breathing. Breathe in through your nose and breathe out through your mouth. Breathe in all the positive energy and breathe out all the negative energy.

Focus your attention on your head. Take time to notice all the sensations in your head. Release all the tension in your head. Release all your worries and aches.

Now, move your attention to your neck and feel all the tension that you've been carrying in the area. Does it itch? Do you feel in the area?

Focus your attention on your shoulder, arms, hands, fingers, elbows, chest, upper back, lower back, abdomen, navel, thighs, knees, legs, ankles, and feet. Notice any sensation or feelings. Do this as slowly as you can. Take time notice any movement, sensation, or pain in each area of your body.

As you examine each part of your body, take time to notice your vulnerable points. Which part of your body is vulnerable to other people's stress and pain? Is it your gut? Is it your head? Is it your neck or your heart? Once you identify your vulnerable point, imagine that there's a bright white light at the top of your head. Imagine that this light is travelling to your pain points, healing them.

Bring your attention back to your breath. Listen to your own heartbeat as your chest rises and falls. Do this for a minute or two.

As you breathe, say this mantra "I release all the pain and tension in my body". Keep breathing. Say a prayer of thanks and then open your eyes.

Get up and move your head, arms, fingers, neck, feet, and toes. Shake off all the tension and pain out of your body.

You can do this meditation technique once or twice a week. You can also do this whenever you feel that you are starting to absorb other people's physical symptoms. It is also helpful to use place a protective stone like an amethyst on your navel while you are doing this.

After this meditation technique, take a shower and rub a bath salt all over your body. This will help cleanse your auric field and remove all the negative energy and physical symptoms that you have absorbed from other people.

Psychic Protection Guided Meditation

This guided meditation protects you from other people's symptoms and negative energy. It helps release stress, too.

To do this, close your eyes and take deep breaths. Breathe in through your nose and breathe out through your mouth. Imagine yourself breathing in pure light and breathing out negative and toxic energy. Do this for around two minutes. Then, visualize an angel above you. This angel has white hair, white wings, and he has a sword. He is your protector. He protects you from diseases, negative energy, and toxic people.

Now, imagine that the angel is sending a light down to you. This light protects you from all the negative energy around you. This light keeps you from absorbing other people's symptoms. This light comforts you in times of fear. This light heals every cell in your body.

Imagine that this light is all around you. No one can harm you. Sickness cannot enter your body. This light keeps darkness and negativity away. Imagine the light growing bigger and bigger.

As you breathe, say "I am guided. I am protected". Repeat this over and over until you feel safe. Open your eyes and go about your day knowing that you are safe and that you are protected.

Clearing and Shielding Meditation

This meditation technique helps you manage your energy. It keeps you from taking other people's pain. It helps you become more aware of how this energy affects you.

Place your hands on your heart. Take deep breaths and connect with your inner self as you breathe in and breathe out. Then, ask yourself, "how am I feeling right now? Do I feel tired? Do I feel happy? Do I feel sick? Am I at peace? Am I in pain?".

Keep breathing and give yourself space to experience different feelings and tensions. Allow these emotions and tensions to come and go.

Imagine that there's a bright green light shining at the center of your chest. This is your heart chakra. Breathe in all the positivity in the world and breathe out all the negative energy and symptoms that you have absorbed from other people. Focus on the light at the center of your chest. If your mind wanders, bring your focus back to your heart chakra.

As you breathe, this brilliant and shimmering green light expands to different parts of your body – your arms, neck, torso, hands, legs, and feet. Imagine that the light is now covering every inch of your body. This light protects you. It creates a barrier between you and the world. This psychic field acts as a shield against all the negative energies vibrating around you. It protects you from other people's symptoms. This light keeps you healthy and safe.

Keep breathing. Always remember that you are protected all the time no matter where you are in the world. You are safe. You are healthy. You are okay.

CHAPTER 6

MEDITATION TECHNIQUES TO OVERCOME FEAR

Fear is crippling. It can affect not just your mind but your body as well. It negatively impacts your decision-making in a lot of ways.

If you live in constant fear, you'll eventually develop mental health issues such as depression, social anxiety, specific phobias, obsessive compulsive disorder, and panic disorder. Fear can wreak havoc in your life because it can keep you from living the life that you truly deserve. It can keep you from doing the things that you really want to do. It can also keep you from going after the things that you really want.

If you're an empath, you'll struggle with fear constantly because of the negative energy that you absorb from other people. You constantly feel anxious and you'll have difficulty sleeping. You'll also experience physical symptoms of fear such as shortness of breath, dizziness, palpitations, cold and sweaty hands, and nausea.

Meditation is a powerful tool that can help eliminate your fears. It helps you drop past baggage that's associated with your fears. It allows you to recognize your fears without emotionally reacting to them. Meditation also reduces the activity in the ventrolateral prefrontal cortex and amygdala, the region in your brain that governs phobias.

Most fears and phobias are linked to past events and experiences. However, a lot of people also fear the future. Meditation helps you overcome these fears by training your mind to live in the present.

Living in the moment can benefit you in a lot of other ways too. It helps you stop fidgeting and nail-biting habit. It helps you become less attracted to escapist entertainment like TV. It helps you curb your cravings. Most of all, it helps you enjoy life more.

Affirmation Meditation to Overcome Fears

When you are an empath, you may have developed fears and phobias over the years through the negative energies that you absorb from other people. You can remove your fears, doubts, and phobias through constant meditation practice.

To do this, sit in a comfortable position. You can sit in a cross-legged position on the floor or you can sit on a chair. Close your eyes and take deep breaths. Focus on your breath and if negative thoughts enter your mind, acknowledge and let go of these thoughts.

Keep taking deep breaths and as you inhale, say these affirmations:

- *I am fearless.*
- *I let go of all my fears.*
- *I am brave.*
- *I can be the best that I can be.*
- *I am confident.*
- *I am strong.*
- *I am determined to achieve my dreams.*
- *I will work hard and face the challenges head on.*
- *I am naturally fearless.*

- *I am not afraid to face the things that I am afraid of.*
- *I persist even when things are tough.*
- *I am motivated to do my best all the time.*
- *I am determined to succeed even when I face problems and setbacks.*
- *I am strong and I can handle anything.*
- *I am powerful, I am not a victim.*
- *I am daring.*
- *I move through my fears.*
- *I act even when I am afraid.*
- *I am getting braver and braver each day.*
- *I let go of all my childhood terrors.*
- *I let go of all my fears.*
- *I take action.*
- *I am unstoppable.*
- *I believe that I can do this.*
- *I let go of my childhood fears.*
- *I create a world that is safe.*
- *I am daring and bold.*
- *I release and I let go of my old fears.*
- *I no longer scare myself.*
- *I forgive the people who hurt me.*
- *I forgive my parents for transferring their fears and limitations to me.*

- *I create a reality of security.*
- *I am safe.*
- *I am at peace.*
- *I live in a safe place.*
- *I do not fear anything.*
- *My life is filled with peace.*
- *I know that I can do anything.*
- *I am strong enough to overcome challenges.*
- *I bravely welcome each day.*
- *I am safe in my home.*
- *I am tough.*
- *I am courageous.*
- *I am not afraid to begin again.*
- *I forgive others and move on.*
- *I am free.*
- *I am safe in buses, cars, skateboards, and bicycles.*
- *I am not afraid to travel and take risks.*
- *I am calm at all times.*
- *I am not afraid to stand up for myself.*

Continue to take deep breaths. Release all your fears as you breathe. Slowly open your eyes.

You do not have to say all these affirmations; you just have to pick the ones that work well for you. You can even create your affirmations. If you find it hard to remember these affirmations, you can simply record yourself saying them. Then, you can play the recording during your meditation session.

Mantra Meditation for Overcoming Your Fears

Sit in a comfortable position. You can spray lavender, rose, bergamot, or ylang ylang oil in the room. These essential oils help you overcome your fears.

Close your eyes and take deep breaths. Focus your attention on your breath. If a distracting thought enters your mind, acknowledge it and let it go. Bring your attention back to your breath.

Imagine that there's a bright white light around you. This white light protects you from all the bad things around you. It protects you from all the negative energy that surrounds you. This light invigorates you, gives you energy, and courage. This light shines around you, protecting you from people who want to harm you. You are protected. You are safe. Nobody can harm you.

Breathe in courage and then breathe out all your fears. Do this for around one minute or two. Now, when you breathe in, say this mantra "Feel the fear and do it anyway". Repeat this mantra as you take a deep breath.

Now, open your eyes and say a prayer of gratitude.

Visualization Meditation to Overcome Your Fears

Visualization is a powerful tool that you can use to overcome your fears and anxiety. It has the strong ability to make you feel safe and at peace. This meditation technique helps cure anxiety and stage fright. It helps you overcome the different types of fear such as fear of rejection, separation anxiety, fear of being restricted, shame, fear of pain, fear of uncertainty, and conditioned fear.

This technique helps build your courage. It gives you strength in times of adversity. This technique increases your self-confidence and strengthens your conviction and determination. It gives you the courage to embrace the unknown and take risks. It also motivates you to take action.

1. To do this, close your eyes and take deep breaths. Focus on your breath. Notice how your chest moves up and down as you inhale and exhale.

2. Imagine yourself sitting on a rock in the middle of a huge jungle. You can see huge trees. You can hear the birds chirping as they are flying above you. Continue to take deep breaths. Now, imagine a bright white light at the base of your spine. This light grows bigger and bigger every time you breathe. This light protects you from all the bad things in this world. This light gives you security. It protects you from all the stress in the world. It keeps you away from harm.

3. Now imagine that there are wild animals around you. There are lions and tigers all around you. Imagine that these wild animals are surrounding you. They're trying to attack you, but the bright white light is keeping them away from you. No matter how hard they try, these wild animals could not get close to you. You are safe. You are invincible. You get up and start walking, not minding all the danger

around you. You are safe. You are secure. No one can harm you.

4. Keep walking until you see the beach at the end of the forest. This beach is a symbol of peace and securities. Listen to the sound of the waves and feel the warmth of the sand under your feet.

5. Feel the white light growing bigger and bigger until it covers everything that you see. You live in the world that is safe. You are protected from the negative energies around you. You are safe. No one could harm you.

6. Now, imagine yourself doing the things that you are afraid to do. Imagine that you are speaking in front of a thousand people. Visualize yourself doing something exciting like zip lining, surfing, or bungee jumping. Imagine yourself confessing your feelings to the person you love the most.

7. Take deep breaths and listen to the sound of your breath. Open your eyes. Do this exercise

whenever you feel anxious and whenever you feel fear.

Basic Mindfulness Meditation for Empaths

This basic meditation technique helps you overcome your fear and anxiety by living in the moment. It reduces the symptoms of stress and it slows down your breathing. It also reduces your emotional reactivity to negative situation and circumstances. It improves your cognitive flexibility and stimulates feelings of satisfaction in your relationship. This simple meditation technique does not only help you overcome fears, it also increases the quality of your life.

1. To do this, sit in a comfortable position. You can sit on a chair or a cushion. Then, start to take deep breaths. Focus on your breath and tune out all your thoughts and worries. Notice how your chest goes up and down as you breathe.

2. If a thought enters your mind, acknowledge it and then, let it go. Do this for around five

minutes. Then, say a silent prayer of thanks and then open your eyes.

You can do this technique five minutes daily during your first week. Then, you can increase your meditation time as you progress.

Fear-Into-Love Meditation

This meditation technique aims to transform fear into love. It aims to transform negative energy into positive energy.

To do this, sit in a quiet place that's free from distractions. Close your eyes and bring your awareness to your breath. Notice how your chest goes up and down as you breathe. Surrender yourself completely to your breath. Relax and guide your body to a deep meditative state.

Imagine that you standing in a middle of a dark, empty room. This room will help you become more grounded and centered. Visualize that you are sending a white light full of energy to the wall in front of you. Now, draw that energy back towards your body. Send that energy to the wall behind you and then, gently pull the energy back into your body.

Send the energy to the wall on your right and then to the wall on your left. Then, draw that energy back. Continue to breathe rhythmically. Surrender your body to every breath. In this moment, there's nothing for you to do but to surrender to your breath. Allow yourself to fall into a trance-like state. In this moment, reflect on the things that you are afraid of. What are you afraid of? Are you afraid of death? Are you afraid of the future? Are you afraid of rejection, of not being good enough? Are you afraid of not measuring up? What experiences made you feel fear? Now, think about the butterflies in your stomach and the emptiness inside. Bring the awareness all the feelings of discomfort associated with your fears.

Think about the things that you are afraid of – rejection, failure, spiders, snakes, and heights.

Then, replace your fear with love. Send love and light to all the things that you are afraid of. Send love to the sources of your anxiety. Transform all your fears, anxieties, and worry into love – for yourself and for others. Change those fears into love. Then, say these affirmations out loud:

- *I love myself.*
- *I accept myself.*
- *I am proud to be myself.*
- *I am proud of who I am and if others don't like me, that's okay.*
- *I will do my best and my best is good enough.*

Continue to take deep breaths. Inhale through your nose and exhale through your mouth. Then, open your eyes and feel all the love around you. You have successfully transformed all your worries and fears into love.

CHAPTER 7

YOGA FOR EMPATHS

Yoga is a moving meditation and it has a powerful calming effect, especially to empaths. It's not just a popular workout for hippies and suburban housewives. It does more than improve your muscle strength or flexibility. Yoga improves your overall mental well-being.

Empaths have a hard time identifying which feelings are theirs and which feelings are not. An empath is usually has an emotional satellite radio that hundreds of channel. The empath's nervous system constantly flips from one station to another to listen to other people's emotional broadcasts and complaints. This is exhausting and over time, this could lead to nervous breakdown.

Some empaths spend years, if not decades, just to master taking control of their emotions. This is the reason why yoga is a powerful elixir for empaths. Yoga silences your mind. It helps you become more aware of who you are and it helps you stay in touch with your own emotions.

Yoga can help empaths in different ways:

1. Yoga helps you process your own emotions.

    If you're an empath, you'll have a hard time separating your own emotions from other people's feelings. Yoga connects your body and mind. It helps you become aware of every nerve and muscle in your body. It also helps you listen to your mind and be more aware of your emotions. It helps you accept your feelings and separate them from other people's emotions.

    A lot of empaths try to downplay their own emotions as less important as other people's feelings. Yoga helps you acknowledge not only your feelings, but also the disturbing sensations that are associated with those feelings.

    If you're depressed, for example, you will feel different body sensations such as headaches, back pain, joint pain, chest pain, fatigue, and sleep disturbances. If you're anxious, you'll feel tingling sensations all over your body. You'll also experience chest pains and numbness. After all, your body can reflect your emotional history. Yoga helps you identify those sensations and process your emotions.

Yoga helps you tune out other people's emotions and be more aware of your own emotions. It helps you identify your anger and the behaviors that are associated with it. It also helps you identify the thoughts that are triggering those emotions.

Yoga is not only a physical exercise. It is a practice that helps you lean into your emotions instead of running away from them or tuning them out. It helps respond proactively to a negative emotion so it does not linger. It allows you to listen to your own emotion, feel its power, accept it, and let it go.

2. Yoga helps release your emotional blockages.

Emotional blockages are typically created by traumatic experiences, self-limiting beliefs, and unresolved emotions. A lot of other things can cause emotional blockages such as financial difficulty and relationship issues. But, empaths can develop emotional blockage just by feeling other people's anguish, disappointment, and pain.

Emotional stress and blockage can cause a lot of health problems. It can lead to depression and mental suffocation. You'll feel anxious all the time and you'd also experience intense headaches from time to time. When you experience emotional stress, you tend to be forgetful and sickly, and you'll have a hard time processing information. You also have a hard time eating or sleeping. You may also feel angry and annoyed by small details.

Yoga helps release trauma, negative experiences, and negative emotions that caused emotional blockage. It also helps balance your emotions and achieve an emotional breakthrough.

3. It clears stagnant and negative energy.

   Yoga is a physical exercise that helps clear out all the negative and stagnant energy. Each movement aims to balance your chi or life energy.

Yoga Types for Empaths

Pranayama

Pranayama is a Sanskrit word that literally means "extension of breath". It comes from two Sanskrit words – prana and ayama. Prana is a life force energy that runs throughout the human body. Ayama, on the other hand, means to draw out. Pranayama is a practice that helps you draw out your life force energy. It is an important part of the yoga system. It is basically the process of controlling your breath.

Pranayama can do a lot of wonders to your health. It reduces your breathing rate and help you relax. It also reduces the wear and tear of your vital organs, improving your overall well-being and health. It improves your blood circulation and it protects you from negative mental conditions such as depression, greed, anger, and arrogance. It even improves memory retention and concentration. It improves your general well-being.

Empaths often find it hard to control their thoughts. They have wandering thoughts. Pranayama helps you control your thoughts. It increases your emotional stability and it helps you ward off negative emotions.

We will discuss this in detail later on.

Restorative Yoga

Restorative yoga is for those who experience intense stress in their lives, like empaths. This yoga type helps clear your mind. It also helps you relax amidst the challenges a turbulence of life.

Restorative yoga encourages mindfulness. Its slow movements cultivate a deeper experience. It encourages mindfulness and it soothes the nervous symptoms. This yoga type heightens your body awareness. It improves your introspection and self-awareness. It also helps you develop detachment.

It strengthens your ability to accept yourself just about you. It enhances your flexibility and it reduces oxidative stress. It also helps you develop patience and increase your self-awareness. Most of all, it heals emotional pain. It is also a good segue to a meditation practice. It is easy and fun, too.

Pranayama for Empaths

As mentioned earlier, pranayama is a powerful technique that helps you relax and ward off toxic energy. There are many pranayama techniques, but the following breathing techniques are best for empaths:

Nadi Shodhana or Alternate Nostril Breathing

This breathing technique is simple yet powerful. It can restore your emotional balance. It calms your mind and helps you develop understanding about yourself. It enhances your mood states and it improves your capacity for healing and balancing your emotions. This technique also helps remove toxins and ease stress.

To do this:

1. Sit in a comfortable position and make sure that your heart is open and your spine is straight.

2. Close your eyes and take deep breaths.

3. Now, place your right thumb on your right nostril. Inhale through your left nostril. Then, place your index finger on your left nostril. Remove your thumb and open your right nostril. Then, exhale through your right nostril.

4. Repeat this process ten to fifteen times daily to reap its full benefits.

This powerful technique has been used in Ayurvedic medicine for a long time. Aside from its relaxing effects, this breathing exercise also improves your fine motor coordination and enhances your respiratory functions.

Kapaphalbati or Bellows Breath

This breathing exercise is powerful and helps you lose weight. Many yoga practitioners claim that this technique is powerful enough to cure various diseases such as constipation, breast cancer, lung problems, kidney stones, and bone problems.

This breathing technique also awakens the ajna chakra. It also releases mental discomfort, stress, and anger. It can do wonders to your skin, too.

1. To do this, sit in the lotus position.

2. Then, close your eyes while keeping your spine aligned.

3. Take a deep breathe through your nose until you feel that your lungs have become full with air. Then exhale through your nostrils with force so that you'll feel your stomach going deep inside.

Yoga Tips for Empaths

Going to group gatherings such as a yoga class can be overwhelming for empaths. If you're one, it is probably a good idea to just practice yoga at home. Make no mistake; attending public yoga classes has a lot of benefits, too. For one, it's important to practice with a certified yoga teacher, especially when you're a beginner. It also helps you build camaraderie with other practitioners and get the much needed support. It is always good to share your yoga journey with people who also go through the same challenges that you go through such as stress, anxiety, or depression.

Here's a list of tips that you can use to get the most out of your yoga practice:

1. Try compassionate detachment.

   Whatever emotions other people feel are not yours to carry. If you're an empath, you'll probably find it hard to see someone feeling intense emotions in the yoga room and not be concerned. But, you have to tell yourself that you are not responsible for other people's emotions. You can still be compassionate but you should not get too attached.

   Remember that those feelings are not yours. This is not to say that you should be a jerk and ignore someone else's pain. After class, you can simply approach the person and tap her shoulder or simply give a reassuring look.

2. Try to be mindful of your location.

   If you are an empath, you don't want to position your yoga mat in the middle of the room where you will be surrounded by people on all sides. When it is possible, it's a good idea to position your yoga mat in the corner of the room or against a window. If there's a plant in the room, you can place your mat near it. This will help calm you down.

3. Wear protective stones.

   To ward off the negative energies in the room, it's a good idea to wear stones that have protective qualities such as amethyst, amber, diamond, emerald, hematite, yellow jasper, lapis lazuli, green apophyllite, aquamarine, lepidolite, aquamarine, obsidian, quartz, black onyx, peridot, quartz, tiger's eye, turquoise, black tourmaline, and black sapphire.

4. If you're on a budget, practice at home.

   Yoga can be expensive. A yoga class typically costs $12. If you decide to do yoga three times a week, it could cost you $144 a month. If you have a tight budget, it's a good idea to attend yoga classes for about a month or two and then, you can do home practice later one. Practicing at home is great for empaths. You can wear whatever you like, you do not have to buy those expensive yoga clothes to keep up with your classmates. Most of all, it keeps you from absorbing the negative energies that other people may carry.

Another advantage of practicing at home is that you get to design your space. It helps you build discipline and most of all, it's free and you get to practice anytime.

5. Practice self-love.

When you're practicing yoga, it is important to be kind to yourself. You have to put yourself and your comfort first. Always listen to your body. Do not do anything that could potentially harm your body. Do only the things that feel good and do not stress over what you look like.

Yoga is a practice that could greatly benefit empaths. It could help you sort out your emotions and it could strengthen your mind and body connection. It also helps you separate your emotions from other people's emotions and energies.

Yoga Poses for Empaths

Child's Pose or Balasana

If you're an empath, you have to constantly deal with mental noise. Child's pose helps you sort out your emotions. It calms your mind and it relaxes your entire body.

To do this, kneel on your yoga mat. Then, bring your upper body forward and place your head on the mat. Stretch your arms above your head, palms down. Stay in this position for two to three minutes.

Corpse Pose or Savasana

This is the easiest yoga pose. It is the most relaxing, too. This pose releases stress and it reduces symptoms of depression, fatigue, stress, and tension. It helps cure depression and it relaxes your muscles. It calms the mind and improves your mental health.

To do this, lie on your back with your arms on the side, palms up. Your legs should be slightly apart. Close your eyes and just relax. Allow your tension and stress to melt away with every breath. Stay in this position for at least 5 minutes and try not to fall asleep.

Happy Baby Pose or Ananda Balasana

The happy baby pose looks funny but it has a lot of benefits. It opens your inner thighs, hips, and groins. It relieves lower back pain and it calms the brain.

Lie on your back. Take a deep breath. Then, bend your knees to your belly. As you breathe in, hold soles of your feet. Keep breathing and touch the soles. Hold this position for a minute or two. Release and repeat.

Legs Up The Wall or Viparita Karani

This pose improves your blood flow and it helps relieve tired leg muscles. It has a calming effect.

It helps remove the symptoms that you have absorbed from other people. It also relieves various diseases such as anxiety, migraines, varicose veins, menstrual cramps, arthritis, muscle fatigue, mild depression, insomnia, and respiratory problems. This pose strengthens your immune system and balances your hormonal system. It also stabilizes your digestive system.

Sit sideways around six inches from the wall. Take a deep breath and swing your legs up to the wall. Keep your legs together and take deep breaths while you are in this position. Hold this pose for thirty seconds to one minute. Keep breathing. Breathe in through your nose and then, out through your mouth. Then, gently bring your legs down.

Reclining Hero Pose or Supta Virasana

This pose is extremely relaxing and it also has a number of therapeutic applications. It can help decrease the symptoms of infertility, cold, headache, digestive problems, ashthma, arthritis, sciatica, and intestinal gas. It strengthens your arches and also improves digestion.

To do this, kneel on your mat. Inhale through your nose and as you exhale, lower your body down to the mat. You should be sitting on the soles of your feet. Place your arms on your side, palms up. Close your eyes and take deep breaths. Hold this pose for thirty to sixty seconds.

Reclining Hand to Big Toe Pose

This pose lowers you blood pressure. It stretches the hips, hamstrings, calves, and groins. It relieves backache, menstrual discomfort, and sciatica. This pose can do wonders to your core muscles, too. It is extremely relaxing.

To do this, lie on your back. Take a deep breath and lift your left leg up, then lift your left arm and try your best to reach your toes. You can bend your knee if you have a hard time doing this. Hold this pose for at least thirty seconds.

Bring your left leg down. Take a deep breath and lift your right leg up. Lift your right arm and try your best to reach your toes. Repeat this process three to five times.

Camel Pose

This pose cleanses your heart chakra and removes all the negative energy and emotions in that area.

To do this, kneel on your yoga mat. Take a deep breath and then lean back. Drop your head down, lift your chest, and touch the soles of your feet. Hold this pose for thirty to sixty seconds.

Low Squat or Malasana

This pose opens your hips and your lower back. It also allows you to release all the negativity in your life. To do this, stand on your mat, legs wide apart. Place your hands in front of you in a prayer position. Then, slowly lower your buttocks down so your hips are hovering above your mat. Hold this pose for about thirty seconds and then, go back to the standing position.

Tree Pose

This pose grounds you and it helps alleviate anxiety. It improves your awareness, focus, and awareness. It improves your balance. To cleanse your energy, perform this pose before each meditation session.

To do this pose, stand tall on your mat. Make sure that your feet are firmly planted on the ground. Then, shift your weight to your left leg and place your right feet on the side of your left knee. Place your hands on top of your head, palms together. Take deep breaths and hold this pose as long as you can.

Put down your right feet and shift your body weight to your right leg. Place your left feet on the side of your right knee. Hold this pose for a few seconds or minutes.

Warrior III

As the name suggests, this yoga pose makes you feel like a warrior. It improves your balance and it helps you shake off all the anxiety from your body. This pose can also do wonders to your core muscles and help eliminate belly fat.

To do this, stand on your yoga mat. Take a deep breath and bring your left leg back. Then, bring your upper body forward. Place your arms in front of you, palms facing each other. Your body should form a "T" shape. Hold this pose for three to five breaths. Go back to standing position.

Take a deep breath and kick your right leg back. Bring your upper body forward and place your arms in front of you. Hold this position for three to five breaths and then release. Repeat this three to five times.

Downward Facing Dog

This pose helps ease anxiety and fear. It rejuvenates your body and reduces fatigue.

To do this, start on all fours. Then, lift your pelvis, knees, stomach and chest up. Plant your feet and hands firmly on the mat. Your body should form a "reverse V" shape. Hold this pose for ten breaths. Release and repeat if necessary.

Bridge Pose

This pose is relaxing. It improves your blood circulation. It helps alleviate mild depression and stress.

To do this, lie on your back. As you breathe, lift your buttocks, chest, and knees from the ground. Place your arms on your side and hold your ankles. Hold this pose for a few minutes.

Yoga improves your health in many ways. It also helps you squeeze out the stagnant energy from your body. Attending yoga classes is a good way to meet other sensitive souls, too.

CONCLUSION

Thank you again for purchasing this book!

Being an empath is tiring. I hope that this book was able to help lift your burdens. I hope the meditation techniques contained in this book helps you achieve that one thing we all desire – peace of mind.

Being an empath can be difficult, but keep in mind that it can also be a gift to the people around you. You are special and strong. You are a valuable person and your needs are important, too.

Take care of yourself by practicing meditation and yoga. Also, make sure to create personal boundaries. There's nothing wrong with empathizing with others. In fact, empathy is important in building genuine relationships. But, you don't need to absorb other people's pain. You don't need to absorb their physical symptoms, worries, and heartaches.

Watch your thoughts closely. When you feel frustrated, ask yourself whether this is your frustration or something that you have absorbed from another person. Do this regularly to avoid bigger problems like depression or mental breakdown.

Always remember this: you are important and you deserve all that is good in this world. You are safe. You are protected. You have the power to filter all the energies that enter your body.

Once again, don't forget to grab a copy of your Free Bonus book *"How to Talk to Anyone: 50 Best Tips and Tricks to Build Instant Rapport"*. If you want to increase your influence and become more effective in your conversations then this book is for you.

Just go to http://ryanjames.successpublishing.club/freebonus/

Thank you and good luck!

Thank you!

Before you go, we just wanted to say thank you for purchasing my book.

You could have picked from dozens of other books on the same topic but you took a chance and chose this one.

So, a HUGE thanks to you for getting this book and for reading all the way to the end.

Now we wanted to ask you for a small favor. **Could you please take just a few minutes to leave a review for this book?**

This feedback will help us continue to write the type of books that will help you get the results you want. So if you enjoyed it, please let us know! (-:

www.ingramcontent.com/pod-product-compliance
Lightning Source LLC
Chambersburg PA
CBHW070042230426
43661CB00005B/723